THE ROYAL LEICESTERSHIRE REGIMENT

AN ILLUSTRATED HISTORY

ROBIN JENKINS & JAMES RYAN

The
History
Press

First published 2013

The History Press
The Mill, Brimscombe Port
Stroud, Gloucestershire, GL5 2QG
www.thehistorypress.co.uk

British Library Cataloguing in Publication Data.
A catalogue record for this book is available from the British Library.

ISBN 978 0 7524 6514 2

Typesetting and origination by The History Press
Printed in Great Britain

CONTENTS

Introduction   5

1   Home Service & the depot at Glen Parva   7

2   'HINDOOSTAN': Service in Afghanistan, India   64
    & Burma

3   North America   84

4   Sevastopol: Service on the Black Sea   93

5   North Africa & the Middle East   97

6   South Africa   111

7   The Western Front: France & Flanders   123

8   Germany   134

9   Italy & Greece   140

10 The Far East: Malaya, Hong Kong, Korea, Brunei   145
    & Borneo (& Australia)

11 Come on the Tigers!   151

    'Wolfe's Dirge'   159

On 27 July 1954, the 1st Battalion, serving with the British Army on the Rhine, received new Colours from the Chief of the Imperial General Staff, Field-Marshal Sir John Harding, at Iserlohn. Here the RSM, 'Tommy' Marston, commands the escort of sergeants J. Parren, K. Colclough and C. Marshall, while Lieutenant M.L. Barclay holds the Queen's and 2nd Lieutenant J.H. Rees the Regimental Colour.

INTRODUCTION

This will not be a conventional history of Leicestershire's regiment of the line. It cannot be. For one thing it is hard – but not impossible – to illustrate a regimental history from 1688 when the earliest photographs we have date from 1855 and cameras, until fairly recently, were excluded from the battlefield either by practicality or military regulations.

A single picture may be worth a thousand words but even so, there are far too few pages here to record, as they deserve, the service and sacrifice of generations of 'Tigers'. Furthermore, the photographic collections of the Record Office for Leicestershire, Leicester & Rutland, rich though they are, inevitably have their gaps and weaknesses. This is especially noticeable for the final decades of the regiment and is a well-known phenomenon in archives – recent archive material is rarely surrendered by families; it is only the remote and near forgotten material which can safely be parted with.

The Colours and drums of the 1st Battalion, 1910.

We, at the Record Office, are always eager to add to our holdings and to make good the deficiencies you may detect here. Besides, photographs can be copied (even enhanced if the know-how and technology is there). If you can help us – we are eager to hear from you.

This is not intended to be just a tale of battles and sieges. Our intention is to chart not only the actions of the Royal Leicestershire Regiment but also the 'family spirit' of those Tigers, their growing traditions and habits, and the place the regiment has in our community. We shall note too the changing appearance of Leicestershire's soldiers – their dress, equipment and weapons; though, on occasion, it is the similarities which will surprise rather than the differences. These images then have been chosen for their quality, for the story they tell, and because they are unfamiliar. We shall also make space for the other members of the regimental family – the militia and volunteers – who were eventually to be absorbed into the Tigers.

I have decided not to follow a strictly chronological course. Partly it is a response to the gaps mentioned above – but also, I prefer to tell the story of our regiment with an eye to its service throughout the world. This is almost a 'family album' of the regiment; a record of travels and triumphs but also sadnesses and everyday life.

We shall begin with home service and then board the transports for 'Hindoostan' (the regiment's honour for time spent in India and Afghanistan). We shall journey to North America and the Caribbean, the Black Sea and Middle East before steaming across the Channel for service on the Western Front and in Germany, Africa and the Far East.

My thanks are due to James Ryan and Julie Thomson for their photographic skill in bringing long-faded images back to 'life', to the Royal Tigers Association (and especially Colonel Anthony Swallow, whose dedication to the regiment's history makes my life as their archivist so much more easy and pleasurable), to Captain Richard Lane, whose enthusiasm for his regiment knows no bounds, and to Jess Jenkins, who is at once my adjutant, drill sergeant and comrade-in-arms.

We shall begin however, as all new recruits do, with the depot and home service.

Robin P Jenkins, Senior Archivist (Collections) Wigston, 2013

1

HOME SERVICE & THE DEPOT AT GLEN PARVA

Leicestershire's county regiment was actually raised in London, by order of James II, in 1688. The practice of the day was to call the regiment after its colonel and so what was eventually to become the Leicestershire Regiment spent its first six months as Colonel Solomon Richards' Regiment of Foot. The following year it became Colonel Sir George St George's Regiment, and so on. In 1751, another royal warrant assigned numbers to regiments (in the order of their raising) and so John Wynard's become the 17th Regiment of Foot.

The first local connection was made in 1782, when (to aid recruitment) the regiment became the 17th (or Leicestershire) Regiment of Foot. In truth, there was little to link county and regiment until 1880, when the barracks at Glen Parva were opened. The following year the Cardwell reforms abolished the 17th Foot; creating in its stead the Leicestershire Regiment.

Although the Tigers saw their fair share of service throughout the Empire, one or other of the two regular battalions was often at home or in Ireland – indeed, the first active service of the regiment was an abortive attempt to raise the siege of Londonderry in 1689. There was fighting too in Scotland in 1715, where a Jacobite invasion was halted at Sherrifmuir.

In the more peaceful nineteenth century, home service was a time for recruitment and training. From 1881 until 1964, the depot at Glen Parva served as home for the Tigers, receiving recruits and sending drafts of trained men throughout the world to wherever the 1st and 2nd Battalions of the regiment were stationed. Glen Parva was home too for the volunteers and kept the regiment at the forefront of local society. For the last four years of its life, the depot housed the Forester Brigade, but closed in 1964 on the formation of the Royal Anglian Regiment.

Taken from the 250th anniversary issue of the regiment's journal, *The Green Tiger*, this trio of an officer, sergeant and private soldier represents the Tigers in their first incarnation of 1688. Solomon Richard's Regiment, as it was known, was to consist of thirteen companies, each of sixty men. Their daily pay varied from the Colonel's £1 (as he received 12s as colonel and 8s as commander of one of the companies) to a sergeant's 1s 6d and a private's 8d. The total cost (per annum) to the government of these forerunners of the Leicestershire Regiment was the princely sum of £16,145 3s 4d. The basic pay of a private in the Royal Anglians is now £17,265.

The Aldershot Coronation Tattoo of 1937. Men of the 2nd Battalion impersonate their counterparts of 250 years before.

More Tigers portraying the 'Blue Company' at the Aldershot tattoo. The men of the regiment were no strangers to costume drama; in 1932 the depot had provided the Roman soldiers for the Leicester Pageant and, as we shall see, reconstructions of past uniforms often featured in celebrations at the depot (and even in India).

Watercolours by the well-known military artist Richard Simkin, portraying a sergeant, officer and private soldier of the 17th Regiment of Foot. Though originally dated to 1807 by Simkin, it would be more accurate to see them as the dress worn by the recruiting company in England as the rest of the regiment was in India in 1807 and unlikely to have adhered so strictly to dress regulations.

An officer wearing his undress uniform and a sergeant in full dress, as they would have appeared in about 1840, both drawn by Richard Simkin.

Two more studies by Richard Simkin. This time the artist has chosen a private of the regiment and a bandsman as his subjects; both from about 1864. Although in the past drummers and musicians often wore uniforms of their regiment's facing's Colour, by the mid-nineteenth century regulations required that all bandsmen wear white, irrespective of regiment.

A BANDSMAN WITH SERPENT 17TH REGIMENT 1830

SEVENTEENTH REGIMENT OF FOOT.

FOR CANNON'S MILITARY RECORDS

Two more uniforms studies from the era just before popular photography. Above, left, is the uniform of a bandsman of the 17th Regiment of Foot in about 1830. The bandsman plays the serpent, which (with its distinctive sound and exotic shape) was popular with military bands from the late eighteenth century onwards. Beside him are two officers on the eve of the Crimean War, as printed in Richard Cannon's history of the regiment.

Above: A remarkable photograph by John Burton showing men of the Leicestershire Militia on parade beside the toll house on the London Road, *c.* 1865. The adjutant, Captain Chester (who served from 1863–5) is mounted in front and Sir Frederick Fowke, also horsed, is to the right. The officers in between are Captains Knight (left) and Archer.

Right: Two militiamen preparing for their regiment's annual muster on the square of the barracks beside the Magazine in Leicester, some time in the 1860s. Trousers and packs have come out of store to be laid carefully on blankets.

Left: This carte-de-visite portrait of Captain G.A. Crickitt from 1867 shows the full-dress uniform of a 17th Regiment officer. The captain's shako, with its white over red ball decoration, sits on the chair beside him.

Below: The 1st Battalion form a square before the gates of Raglan Barracks, Devonport, early in 1867. Against cavalry, or an enemy armed only with spears, the square was still a potent battlefield formation.

The band of the 17th Regiment, at Fort Regent, Jersey, on 24 September 1869.

The officers of the 17th Foot, photographed on the same day. The regiment's commanding officer, Colonel Alexander McKinstry, sits with his arms folded. To the left of McKinstry is Captain A.A. Ross, the regiment's paymaster, while the adjutant, Lieutenant W.M. Rolph, reclines at his feet.

Two views from the late 1860s of the Leicestershire Militia on parade in Leicester's market place. A surviving orderly book from the 1850s shows the organisation of the annual twenty-eight days' training. The muster would begin with a flurry of activity at the Magazine, where the permanent staff of the militia would prepare the muster roll, and see that uniforms and equipment were ready. The arriving militiamen were billeted throughout Leicester, gathering each day for parade and two hours' drill at 8.30 a.m. and 1 p.m. Drill was conducted at The Newarke, Market Square, Market House, Militia Barracks and in better weather, on the racecourse. There were church parades on Sundays and even lessons in reading and writing from the Rector of St Martin's.

The permanent staff of the Leicestershire Militia, photographed in front of the regiment's offices on Magazine Square, Leicester. The medals worn here speak of a wealth of military experience, in the Crimea and India. At the centre sits the adjutant who (at this time) was Captain R.V.S. Grimston, a veteran of the relief of Lucknow and (from 1876) Chief Constable of Leicestershire.

The officers of the Leicestershire Militia, photographed in about 1870 – possibly at the castle in Newark-on-Trent. The army reforms of 1881 were to see the militia transformed into the 3rd Battalion of the Leicestershire Regiment.

This is an intriguing picture. The central figure, staring grimly ahead, with his finger in a book, seems to be Major A. Utterson, who served many years with the 1st Battalion. The Glengarry caps of the drivers of the regimental transport appeared in regulations in 1868, so, if we assume from the dress that the photograph was not taken in India, this group can only date between 1868 and 1870, when the 1st Battalion was in Ireland.

A Colour party outside the brigade depot, *c*. 1885. The barracks at Glen Parva became the Brigade Depot of the 27th Brigade on 26 May 1880. The depot was home to both battalions of the 17th Regiment and also the 45th Regiment, as well as militia, yeomanry and volunteers from Leicestershire and Nottinghamshire.

Two portraits of William Dalrymple Tompson. The first shows Tompson as a major, which was his rank at the time he assumed command of the 1st Battalion in 1879. Tompson had been commissioned into the 17th Foot in 1852 and was one of a draft which joined the regiment in the Crimea in January 1855. Here he wears the British and Turkish Crimean Medals, with the French medal of a Knight of the Legion of Honour. He retired from the army in 1884 but in 1912 was appointed to the honorary position of Colonel of the Regiment, which he held until his death in 1916. The second portrait shows Tompson in civilian dress, perhaps after his retirement.

As we have seen, in 1881 the Leicestershire Militia became the 3rd Battalion of the Leicestershire Regiment. Here Captain Frederick Fowke, photographed in 1886, shows the new uniform of the 3rd Battalion. The Fowkes family had provided several officers for the militia, Frederick's father appearing on parade with the militia in Leicester on page 13.

A beautifully posed group of officers of the 1st Battalion at Aldershot in 1885. Colonel Archibald Hammond Utterson, who assumed command of the battalion the year before, is at the centre wearing his Crimean and Afghan war medals. Utterson served thirty-three years with the Tigers and twenty years after this photograph was taken became the Regiment's (Honorary) Colonel.

It must have taken astounding powers of persuasion to convince the officers of the 1st Battalion to don the uniforms and wigs of their counterparts of two centuries before. The bi-centenary of the regiment was celebrated with a fancy dress ball at York's Assembly Rooms, on 6 January 1888. The Officers of the 3rd Battalion wore the uniform of 1788 and a guard of honour dressed in a mixture of old uniforms was present to meet the guests as they arrived.

The staff sergeants and other permanent staff of the 3rd Battalion, photographed in Magazine Square, Leicester, *c.* 1890. Though some of their children are present, there are no wives in this photograph. The census reveals a thriving community in the old militia barracks, with the birthplaces of both wives and children revealing a trail of garrisons and military stations throughout the Empire.

Richard Simkin's depiction of the new dress regulations of 1903, as worn by the Leicestershire Regiment. There is a new khaki undress uniform and greatcoat, as well new hats and details for cuffs and skirts of the review order tunic.

Opposite, top: This is a fascinating record of drill, presumably at Glen Parva. Here the 3rd Battalion, or perhaps 1st (Volunteer) Battalion, with its band, practice under the watchful, if not critical, eyes of their children. For a brief moment the photographer has proved distraction enough for these army offspring.

Opposite, bottom: In 1906 the 1st Battalion returned home from India. The battalion had been away since 1888, having served throughout the South African War and before that in Bermuda and the West Indies. The 'survivors', who had left with the battalion and returned with it, were few enough for an informal group photograph. They included Lieutenant-Colonel G.H.P. Burne and Captain & Quartermaster J.H. Greasley (at the centre of the front row).

Major Glossop (seated, in mufti) with the Regimental District Football Club, 1907. The depot teams always participated with success in local sporting contests, as their trophies attest. Two of the team are wearing the short-lived, rather unpopular, German-style Broderick cap.

The best shots of the 1st Battalion, 1908. If any lesson was learnt from the Boer War of 1899–1902, it was the importance of marksmanship. Here, resplendent in their shining bandolier equipment (another innovation of the Boer War) is the team which ran the 2nd Devons a close second in the Queen Victoria Cup competition of the Army Rifle Association. Colour-Sergeant W. Armston (the battalion's crack shot and winner of that year's Roupell Cup) stands fourth from left in the rear rank, beside Lieutenant P.H. Creagh.

More victims of the Broderick cap – in this case cooks and signallers of the 2nd Battalion at Colchester in 1905. Named after William St John Broderick, the Secretary of State for War from 1900–3, the caps were of blue cloth, with a white patch behind the cap badge. They swiftly disappeared from the army, surviving with the Royal Marines and many local fire brigades. The signallers (below) have the tools of their trade: signalling lamps, heliographs, semaphore flags in blue and white, and the telescopes with which to read the answers to their messages.

The end of an era. The staff of the Leicester Military District on the eve of its abolition in 1908. The old militia and volunteers were to disappear and the Territorial Force, better suited, it was hoped, for a continental war, was formed in their place.

The 1st Battalion, led by its band, parades through Aldershot where it was stationed from 1910 until 1912.

Two views of the Magazine, the old armaments store of the Leicestershire Militia, from The Newarke (above) and Oxford Street (below). Originally conceived in the 1850s as the home for the county militia, in 1908 the barracks and depot on Magazine Square expanded until (by the time of the photograph below) it was the headquarters not only of the 4th Battalion of the Leicestershire Regiment but also that of the Leicestershire Yeomanry, and local Territorial Army units of the Royal Army Service Corps and Royal Army Medical Corps.

The 1st Battalion receives new Colours from the Duchess of Rutland at Shorncliffe on 31 July 1908. The duchess received in return a diamond brooch in the shape of a tiger, presented by the officers of the battalion. The old Colours were laid up the following year in what was eventually to become the cathedral, in Leicester.

Two more views of the ceremony at Shorncliffe on 31 July 1908. Above, the Duchess of Rutland struggles against the breeze to hand over the new Regimental Colour, while Colonel G.H.P. Burne (beside the drums) stares rigidly ahead. The stocky figure to the left of the group is Major Blackader. Below is the Band of the 1st Battalion, no doubt including in its repertoire the then regimental march 'Romaika', and its traditional accompaniments '1772' and 'We'll all go a-hunting today'.

Despite the damage to this photograph it remains an important record of the 1st Battalion on parade at Shorncliffe in 1910. Such parades, with red tunics and blue helmets, were soon to be a thing of the past.

As this postcard's caption tells us, here is the 1st Battalion at rest in Lechlade during the manoeuvres of 1909. In the foreground Colonel H.L. Croker smokes his pipe while Major Blackader hoists up his trousers and Major Glossop (in between) looks on. Behind them is the battalion transport.

Left and below: In this photograph from the depot at Glen Parva, Colour-Sergeant Bertie Alfred Cook casts a critical eye over a well-turned out old soldier, resplendent with South African War medals and several long-service and good conduct stripes. They are models of what a good soldier should be and were indeed used as such, as the next image shows. Here, the artist Ernest Ibbetson has adapted Colour-Sergeant Cook and his friend to produce the Leicestershire Regiment card in Gale & Polden's 'History and Traditions' series.

Men of the 1st Battalion snatch a few moments of rest during brigade training in 1911. The battalion was stationed at Aldershot, the 'Home of the British Army', which enabled training and manoeuvres at brigade, division and (in 1913) even army corps strength.

Training for the territorials was rarely on so grand a scale. Once a year, for their summer camps, the Leicestershire Territorials (infantry, local army service corps, and sometimes artillery and medical staff) would train together. Here, riding behind the band is Lieutenant-Colonel C.F. Oliver (right), with his adjutant, Captain Olivier, also mounted, at Lovesgrove Camp, Aberystwyth, in July 1912.

The maxim machine guns of the regiment's territorial battalions at High Tor, Whitwick, for their summer camp in 1911 and another camp (below). The heavy, horse-drawn carriages, though useful to carry the guns and their ammunition, had already proved vulnerable at Ladysmith, in October 1899, where the 1st Battalion was forced to abandon a gun when its mule was either killed or stampeded by enemy fire and the carriage proved too awkward to be recovered by its crew.

Although soccer was played by all battalions (even in India) with enthusiasm and success, rugby was the true sport of the 1st Battalion. As Lieutenant Dods noted: 'The Tigers are a team that will go far . . . they took the field clad all in their white with the Bengal tiger badge in the jersies . . . they at once struck the eye as a big, strapping, useful lot, many of them six-footers, and all lithe and hefty.'

The King's Guard, 1912. On 15 May 1912 the 1st Battalion had the honour of providing a guard for King George V, who was staying at the Royal Pavilion in Aldershot. The guard, of two sergeants, two corporals, one bugler and eighteen privates is seen here behind Lieutenant W.H.G. Dods.

Napoleon's army may have marched on its stomach, but the British army of 1912 certainly marched on its feet! While at Aldershot the battalion had enthusiastically competed for the Evelyn Wood Trophy. These photographs pre-date the 1913 re-organisation of the 1st Battalion from eight companies to four and show Lieutenant H.S. Pinder's 'E' Company (above) and Captain T.N. Puckle's (below).

Two more snapshots of the regiment's competitors in the 1911 Evelyn Wood competition. Despite advancing age (he first saw active service in the Crimea) and an outmoded affection for cavalry, Wood's period as Quartermaster General, Adjutant General and commanding at Aldershot and in Southern Command, saw a number of innovations in training. The Evelyn Wood competitions combined marksmanship and marching – so these views of each company's marksmen on the eve of the First World War mark a significant stage in the reform of the army as it learned the lessons of South Africa. Above is 'A' Company and below, 'B'.

Representatives of two more companies (in this case 'D' and 'F') set out in pursuit of the Evelyn Wood trophy. These photographs capture the essence of the old professional army, which was to disappear forever at Ypres and around Loos over the winter of 1914/15. Here is a mixture of fresh-faced youths and whiskery veterans; their tiger badges and boots shining and their rifle-slings 'Blancoed' to perfection.

Drafts of men for Leicester's territorial battalion, the 4th, leave the city in 1914. The crowds have turned out to watch but do not seem to find it anything but a sombre occasion. Low levels of recruitment in the city were a cause of concern to the authorities in 1914, perhaps as many men who had been unemployed for months on end found work in the suddenly booming factories and preferred the certainty of work to the vagaries of military life.

A rare view of the depot at Glen Parva, *c.* 1914, as Major Stoney Smith presents long-service and good conduct medals – a happier occasion than the grim surroundings might suggest.

Lads of the newly raised 8th Battalion at Aldershot in September 1914. As Lieutenant C.A.B. Elliott noted in his diary, 'All the men were in mufti, except a very few who had signed on for a long period, and were given khaki. The mufti soon wore out and for a short time certain vigorous physical exercises were out of the question as the lower garments couldn't bear the strain. The blue (Post Office) or Kitchener's blue was shortly issued much to everyone's disgust.'

The 1st Battalion was at Fermoy, with detachments at Bantry and Berehaven, when the mobilisation telegram reached them on 4 August 1914. No fewer than 579 reservists were called up to bring the battalion up to strength and on 15 August they sailed on three transports from Queenstown to join the 6th Division at Cambridge. Here, the troops (with their rifles and equipment) cram the deck of the steamer *Londonderry*. *(Courtesy: Squire de Lisle)*

Having spent nearly a month near Cambridge, the 1st Battalion finally received orders for embarkation on 7 September 1914. Here troops board the *Braemar Castle*, en route for St-Nazaire.

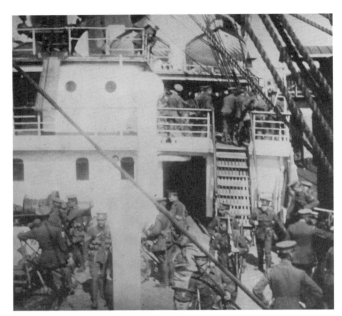

Another snapshot of the 1st Battalion aboard the *Braemar Castle* at Southampton, awaiting their departure for France on 8 September. The battalion was to be rushed south-east through France, where the Germans were at last being pushed back by the French counter-attack on the Marne. The scene is observed by Captain Tideswell, the battalion's adjutant, standing with his back to the camera.

A sergeant of the regiment dressed in breeches and spurs for mounted duty. Although the 1st Battalion had deployed mounted infantry against the Boers in 1899 and mounted infantry training had been carried out by the 2nd Battalion in Egypt in the aftermath of the South African War, the battalions sent to France were purely infantry – save for their transport, much of which was horse-drawn. Possibly our unknown sergeant is from that section; certainly his mount was chosen more for its sturdy constitution than good looks!

Another draft of territorials or reservists march up Leicester's Newarke Street on their way from the Territorial Association offices at the Magazine towards the railway station, in the autumn of 1914.

Ready and equipped for active service, the 7th (Service) Battalion march into Andover (where they are to be billeted), 1915.

The outbreak of war, with its sudden demand for more troops and the experienced men to train and lead them, led to the recall of many who had recently retired from the army. One of those recalled was Lieutenant-colonel J. Mosse, who returned to take command of the depot. Mosse is seen here with his wife and daughter (Sheila) and his two orderlies. It seems likely that Mosse wore himself out coping with the unprecedented demands of the war. Recruitment was alarmingly low in Leicester and the surrounding area compared to neighbouring counties. In early 1915 Mosse was forced to send out recruiting parties beyond Leicestershire in order to satisfy War Office targets. In June 1916 Colonel Mosse died suddenly from a seizure.

Colonel Mosse's funeral was held on 22 June, on the same day that Leicester turned out *en masse* to commemorate Lord Kitchener, whose drowning had seemed so shocking a fortnight before. The crowds from the Kitchener memorial service tramped silently from the town hall and St Martin's Church to follow the band and troops from the depot as they marched to Leicester's Welford Road Cemetery to bid farewell to their former commandant. As F.P. Armitage recalled in his study, *Leicester 1914-1918*, 'It was, in truth, a day of mourning for Leicester. The "Last Post" at St Martin's, the volleys over the grave, formed the background of many a haunting memory, of husband, son, or brother . . .'

There is more than a hint of mischief in this group of band boys, *c.* 1920. The variety of instruments shows how versatile the band had to be, providing music for dances and garden parties, as well as concerts and parades. The battalion is unknown, though it may be the 51st (Young Soldiers).

In 1922 the 1st Battalion was one of the last four British infantry battalions to leave the newly created Irish Free State. For a few months before they had camped in Dublin's Phoenix Park, having handed their barracks at The Curragh over to Irish troops. The camp was kept clean and healthy by the 'Sanitary Squad', snapped here in their working dress and with the tools of their trade.

In December 1921 agreement was reached to establish the Irish Free State. A year later British troops left southern Ireland, the 1st Battalion marching through Dublin to embark for England on 12 December. The stay in Ireland had not been a happy one, with several soldiers shot down in the street, and even the wife of the commanding officer, Colonel Challenor, ambushed and wounded as she drove through Athlone.

The Army Cup final of 1927 brought a triumph for the 2nd Battalion team who beat the Royal Army Ordnance Corps Southern Command (South) team 2–1 at Aldershot. The three 2nd Battalion players to the left of the goalkeeper are Brown, Smith, and Bentham.

The band of the 2nd Battalion at Catterick Camp, 1930.

The 4th Battalion's summer camp at Castle Rock, Whitwick, 1929. Although of dubious military value, the three-legged race was at least enjoyable and must have developed some sense of co-operation!

Health and safety regulations are nothing new. Here the Fire Piquet turns out for a fire drill at the depot, 1930. The walls of the barracks, built in the 1870s, are already ivy-clad and captured German guns adorn the square.

The machine gunners of 'D' Company, 2nd Battalion, winners of the Northern Command Fire Control Cup, 1931.

A recruiting march through Leicester by the 4th Battalion, the city's territorial infantry battalion, 1934.

Physical fitness was, obviously, always important. Here a squad at the depot demonstrates how the trained soldier can defy gravity, June 1936.

Above: A day on the firing range at Kibworth, 28 June 1936. Seated and on the telephone is Major J.F.A. Pitcairn MC. Major F.E. Oliver stands to the left holding a rifle, while 2nd Lieutenant E.J. Cole is between them chewing upon his pipe.

Right: Lieutenant-colonel Alfred Halkyard MC, photographed, probably, in Magazine Square, Leicester, while officer commanding the 4th Battalion, 1932.

Left: Captain J. Withers, MC, DCM, who retired on 17 december 1929 after thirty-eight years with the regiment. He served throughout the South African War and First World War (as his medals attest) and was commissioned from the ranks as Quartermaster of the 4th Battalion.

Below: As part of the regiment's 250th anniversary celebrations, a 'Patriot' class express passenger locomotive was christened *The Leicestershire Regiment.* Brigadier B.C. Dent, seen here with a representative of the LMS Railway, 'launched' the locomotive with a bottle of champagne at the London Road station in Leicester.

Right: Brigadier B.C. Dent, a veteran of Ladysmith (where he had served with the Mounted infantry Company) aboard *The Leicestershire Regiment* at Leicester, 8 July 1938.

Below: Driver T.A. Green and Fireman G. Clements aboard the newly christened and suitably decorated locomotive. Both Green and Clements had served with the regiment during the First World War.

Representatives of the regiment in its various uniforms from 1688 until the 1890s bring on the Tigers' birthday cake, at the Glen Parva officers' 'at home', 5 July 1938.

Lady Woodward, wife of Major General Sir Edward Woodward (Colonel of the Regiment and whose military service had begun with the 2nd Battalion in 1882) attacks the fortified 250th birthday cake, decorated with the Tigers' battle honours.

The five smiling representatives of the Tigers (now freed from cake-carrying duties) in the dress, respectively, of 1688, 1750, 1790, 1800, and 1890.

Celebrations of the 250th anniversary spread throughout Leicestershire. Here, in Market Harborough, on 4 July 1938, the 2nd Battalion is inspected by the Deputy Lieutenant of the County, Brigadier J.L. Jack.

On 7 July 1938, also as part of the 250th anniversary commemoration, the 44th (Leicestershire Regiment) Anti-Aircraft Battalion, Royal Engineers (TA) was inspected on Victoria Park by the Lord Mayor of Leicester.

Welcomed to the depot's 250th anniversary celebrations by Lieutenant-Colonel M.K. Wardle DSO, MC, were two pensioners of the Chelsea Hospital. Both pensioners wear their South African War medals. On the right is Corporal Shread, who (as Drummer Shread) abandoned his drum to the Boers in 1899, only for it to be returned to the regimental museum years later!

At the centre of this photograph of the 2nd Battalion team for the quarter-final of the Army Rugby Cup, 1938, are two of the regiment's international players – Lieutenants A.L. Novis (holding the ball) and D.A. Kendrew, seated next to him on the right.

Postcard photograph of Private John 'Dixie' Dean, with his two mates, Harold Goode and Tom Gamble of 'C' Company, 5th Battalion on guard duty at Thursley Camp, summer 1938. The three are in fighting order, with bayonets fixed and respirator cases.

This parade in their drill hall, on 12 June 1939, shows the effect of the sudden expansion of Leicester's territorial battalion. The demands of modern warfare had already seen the conversion of the old 4th Battalion to an anti-aircraft role. Here they are as the 376th Searchlight Battery, Royal Artillery.

There has always seemed a tendency for armies to prepare for the next war as though it will be the same as the last. Here the 8th Battalion (re-named as the 1st after the fall of Singapore and the capture of the pre-war 1st Battalion) trains to overcome barbed-wire entanglements, 'somewhere in England', c. 1943.

Following the debacle of Norway and the fall of France in 1940, the army prepared first for the defence of the British Isles and then, as 1942 gave way to 1943, for the invasion of the Continent. A seventh battalion was raised in July 1940 and the 50th (Holding) Battalion was redesignated firstly as the 8th and then the 1st Battalion. Both new battalions were posted to coastal defence, to Teeside and Norfolk respectively. These press photographs recall the days of recovery in 1941 and 1942 – not only in confidence but also in equipment and expertise.

Above: As recent experience with security at the Olympics has shown, troops are always useful in domestic emergencies. Here No. 5 Platoon of the depot's 'B' Company pause in their snow clearing near Matlock; probably during the seemingly endless winter of 1947.

Left: No battalion went through more changes than the 4th Battalion. In 1936 they became a searchlight battalion, first with the Royal Engineers and then Royal Artillery. In 1942 they changed again, to become a light anti-aircraft regiment; serving in Normandy and then Holland. Here their old infantry Colours are safely conveyed to the cathedral in Leicester on 15 August 1941.

The Tigers cap badge is unmistakeable but these are gunners of the 579 (Royal Leicestershire Regiment) Light Anti-Aircraft Regiment, Royal Artillery (TA); they may be Royal Artillerymen but they retain the buttons and badges of the Leicestershire Regiment! Above are some of their vehicles on their way to Tonfanau Camp in North Wales, in July 1952. Below is one of the Bofors guns of 'Q' (Royal Leicestershire Regiment) Battery, 438 LAA Regiment at Towyn in 1956.

Athletics remained an important part of the training and welfare programme. Sports at the depot (as well as here with the 1st Battalion in 1953) always managed to mingle competition with enjoyment. In the 1900s there were pillow fights on poles and the married families' race (requiring a wife to run 30 yards to her husband, light his cigarette, and then both to race back – keeping the cigarette alight). In 1953, Major Watson narrowly beat Sergeant E. Johnson to the tape despite the hampering effects of their sacks.

Alderman Miss May Goodwin MBD, JP, Lord Mayor of Leicester inspects Namur Squad on 2 December 1961, one of the last to be trained at Glen Parva. In August the following year the defence minister, John Profumo, announced the end of the Forester Brigade, and the intention, eventually, to close the depot.

The depot's last Christmas dinner, December 1962. Following a long established custom, the officers and warrant officers attended the men's dining hall to serve and see that all went well. Here, Company Sergeant Major Sprason pours the last of a jug of beer into the glass of Private Swinfield. There is little sign that the Forester Brigade (and with it, the Glen Parva barracks) have only another five months left.

2

'HINDOOSTAN':
SERVICE IN AFGHANISTAN,
INDIA & BURMA

The cap badge of the Royal Leicestershire Regiment, which can be seen in so many of these photographs, illustrates perfectly the powerful link between the Tigers and India. The tiger and 'Hindoostan', which arches above it, both testify to the connection, having been awarded in 1825 'as testimony of the exemplary conduct of the corps during the period of its service in India, from 1804 to 1823'. In fact, soldiers of the Leicestershire Regiment were present on the Indian sub-continent for just over half the 143 years from 1804 until the end of the Raj in 1947.

There was fierce fighting on the plains against the Mahrattas in the 1800s and 1820s, in Nepal in 1814, and on the North-West Frontier in the 1930s. Twice the Tigers served in Afghanistan, in 1839 and from 1878 to 1881, and in 1888 the 2nd Battalion took part in the expedition from India into Burma.

The 1st Battalion returned to India in 1902, after the signing of Peace in South Africa. They remained in India until 1906, when (for a brief period of fraternal celebration) they shared stations with the newly arrived 2nd Battalion. The 1st Battalion did not return until 1937, though they made up for their absence with a posting to Razmak on the North-West Frontier, where they saw bitter fighting with the local tribesmen.

The 2nd Battalion occupied a number of Indian postings from 1906 until 1914, when they were mobilised for service in Europe. In 1919 they returned to India from the Middle East, staying until 1923. They were to return once more, with the 7th Battalion, in 1944 and were one of the last British regiments to leave in 1947.

Service in India provided valuable training for the minor wars of empire. However, service there was more often peaceful and though the climate took its toll, life in the cantonments of Jubbulpore or Lucknow had its attractions. Army pay went a long way in India and regimental life continued despite the heat, with sports and gymkhanas, site-seeing and recreation of all kinds. The Leicestershire Regiment's relationship with India and Pakistan remains strong to this day.

The Afghan fortress of Ghuznee was stormed at daybreak on 23 July 1839. Commanding the road to Kabul, Ghuznee was an inevitable target of the British and East India Company force commanded by Sir John Keane, which intended to topple the hostile Afghan ruler Dost Mohammad and to replace him with the more obliging Shah Shuja. Above we see the 2nd and 17th Regiments rushing the blown-in Cabul Gate. Once inside the fortress, the Tigers fought their way along the ramparts and streets beneath to the citadel, where (in the scene below) a brief parley resulted in the surrender of Ghuznee to Lieutenant-Colonel William Croker. The seizure of so strong a fortress resulted in the issue to all ranks of a special campaign medal, only the second general medal issued to British soldiers (the first being the Waterloo Medal).

The 1st Battalion on parade behind Lieutenant-Colonel A.H. Cobbe at Lucknow in 1872. The band (in white) and drums can be seen to the right (our left) of the eight companies. There is no concession to the climate in the dress, which is exactly as worn in Devonport five years before. Careful scrutiny will reveal a sprinkling of Crimea and Canada General Service medals.

The Colours of the 1st Battalion in India, c. 1875. The rifles here are Snider-Enfields, which were not replaced (with Martini-Henry rifles) until 1877. The tunic cuffs are those of the 1871 pattern. These are old soldiers, one sporting three long-service stripes and all wearing their Crimea medals.

A company of the 1st Battalion, photographed in front of their barracks at Lucknow in 1873. The photograph is a fascinating one and repays careful study. Three band boys, in their white uniforms, sit in the front row (inset). Behind them is their officer. Further to the left is an old warrior, standing firmly to attention. He has long-service stripes (each representing two years' service without misconduct, and earning an additional penny's pay each day) and both British and Turkish Crimean medals.

The officers' mess of the 1st Battalion, at Peshawar, in 1875. Clearly, if photography is awkward inside, it is a simple matter to carry the furniture and carpet outside, where the light is better. Here, Colonel Cobbe (with white hair, seated beside Major Utterson) and his officers demonstrate a variety of undress uniforms and mufti.

Subalterns of the 2nd Battalion with their dogs, at Lucknow, c. 1885. To the left stands Lionel Copley Sherer, who was eventually to command the 1st Battalion on the retirement of Colonel Burne in 1908.

Once regimental duty was done for the day, life in India could be leisurely in the extreme. Here, Captain John Mosse and his friends, R.L. Sandwith and B.C. Humfrey of the 17th Regiment, relax on the veranda of their bungalow, at Musheerabad, in 1879. They are joined by G.D. Carleton, who was to command the regiment in South Africa twenty years later, recently arrived from Afghanistan.

Although the faces do not suggest a convivial atmosphere, we may attribute this perhaps to the need for complete stillness during a long, photographic exposure rather than social awkwardness. Here, at Jhansi on 1st October 1881, the station's officers and wives stand or sit in the centre, while three Indian servants (and one long-serving soldier) stand to the side and rear. At the time, the 1st Battalion was divided, with detachments at Gwalior and Nowgong and the headquarters at Jhansi.

Men of the 1st Battalion, with
comrades from the 45th Sikhs
and 2nd Ghurkas, awaiting
the arrival of the Afghan
peace envoys at Gundamak,
Afghanistan. This image
repays careful study. Seated in
the foreground is the bearded
Lieutenant-Colonel
A.H. Utterson, with Generals
J.A. Tytler and Sam Browne
(designer of the famous belt)
behind. Lost among the rocks are
bandsmen of the 17th Regiment
and one soldier from the intended
guard of honour – dressed in red.

Life in India in 1905 had much to recommend it. Here, the sergeants' mess of the 1st Battalion plays host at a picnic, with gramophone, banjo and mandolin for music and football for the more energetic. The regiment's magazine, *The Green Tiger*, shows the sergeants' mess at Belgaum to have been a social hub with dances, sporting competitions and parties of all sorts. The blazers, with matching cap, in Regimental Colours, must have been a local tailor's speciality.

A more significant photograph than its quality might suggest, this snapshot records the departure of the 2nd Battalion from Ranikhet for the Western Front, on 5 September 1914. Within hours of mobilisation on 9 August, the battalion was medically inspected, its bayonets sharpened and boots hobnailed. On 21 September they sailed for Marseille.

The Officers' Farewell Dance, held on leaving Ambala in 1933 was enlivened by this trio – recreating the dress of the regiment's drummers from a century before. Here (left to right) in the Light Company uniform of the 1830s are drummers Taylor, Hallam and Glover.

A military funeral at Multan, 1935. In India, the threat of death was ever present. One private of the 1st Battalion, Teagh, drowned while bathing. Others simply succumbed to the climate or to disease.

Life in British India had its compensations, however. Entertainment was cheap and a host of servants could be retained to carry out routine tasks from shaving to laundering of uniforms, even on army pay in the 1930s.

Church parade for the 1st Battalion at Dalhousie in 1935. The hill station provided a relief from the heat of the plains in summer, though cramped accommodation meant that the battalion's companies 'rotated' there; two companies, with signallers, transport, etc. remaining in Multan.

The 1st Battalion, drawn up for the Proclamation Parade at Multan, 1935. Major Yalland DSO is mounted to the fore, with band and drums to the left. It is well worth comparing this parade to that on page 66, some sixty years earlier.

Removal to the cool heights of Dalhousie in 1935 offered the 1st Battalion training opportunities as well as relief from the heat. Here, some 'tribesmen' of 'A' Company masquerade as 'the enemy' so that their sceptical chums (behind them) can practice the 'open warfare' of the North-West Frontier.

The 1st Battalion cross-country team, runners-up in the Lahore District run, 1934. Seated at the centre are Major R.R. Yalland DSO and Captain A.G. Raleigh MC. The team captain, 2nd Lieutenant I.E.N. MacDougal, is to the left of Yalland.

The 1st Battalion's band hockey team, at Kasauli, *c.* 1937. Fortunately most are identified: (left to right) A.S. Pollard, R.W. Jackson, T. Bradshaw, J. Tether and front F.A. Parker, G. Box, H.J. Wheatley, C.P. Davenport, D. Robbins and A. Coldren.

The army in India was part of a community and supported a way of life centred upon the cantonments. Here, two servants of the 2nd Battalion ensure that standards are maintained even as the Raj comes to an end.

On 2 March 1938, the regiment celebrated the 250th anniversary of its formation. In India the 1st Battalion paraded before the Viceroy and received new Colours. The old Colours are seen here with their escort. On the left is Sergeant J. Meredith who, as RSM Meredith, was to play a vital role in preserving the morale of the 1st Battalion during their years as captives of the Japanese.

The celebrations held in India for the regiment's 250th anniversary included the presentation of new Colours to the 1st Battalion by the Viceroy, the Marquis of Linlithgow.

No. 1 Guard marches past the Viceroy under the command of Captain Harvey. Lieutenants Wills-Rust and Field carry the new Colours, 2 March 1938.

His Excellency the Viceroy of India, with officers of the 1st Battalion at Jubbulpore, 2 March 1938. Seated to the left of the Viceroy is Lieutenant-Colonle H.S. Pinder MC and to his right Major Herring-Cooper. Behind is the turbaned figure of an Indian Army officer, 2nd Lietunenat Kharta Singh, on attachment to the Battalion.

The mule train of the 2nd Battalion, snapped by Captain Ralph Leyland, one of the battalion's transport officers, c. 1944. In the harsh conditions of the Burmese jungle, the pony and mule-borne supplies proved vital.

'Now you shock troops, superbly equipped are going in to beat the Japs.' A view of the 7th Battalion's introduction to jungle warfare. In 1943 they joined the 2nd Battalion in preparations for long-range penetration into Japanese-held territory, in an effort to stem the enemy advance towards India. Although he was killed before the operation could begin, its originator, Orde Wingate, did much to convince his troops that the mountains and jungle of Burma were, in fact, no less hostile to the Japanese as they seemed to the British. The dry humour of this forgotten army appears here in their depiction of a smartly dressed staff officer, assuring them that the seemingly invincible enemy could in fact be beaten.

Opposite: More snapshots of the 2nd Battalion in Burma with the mule train and evacuation of the wounded. Some five officers and sixty men of the regiment gave their lives in Burma in 1944 and 1945. Even just living, let alone fighting in the tropical climate and across a terrain as cruel as the enemy, made the lot of these soldiers a harsh one.

Another of Captain Leyland's snapshots from the 2nd Battalion's campaign beyond the Chindwin River in Burma. Although troops could be supplied with ammunition and American 'K' rations by air, the conditions on the ground dictated that only the lucky few (if the wounded or sick could be termed 'lucky') could be evacuated by Stinson light aircraft.

Casting off an empire could often be as bloody a business as winning one. Riots in Bombay in September 1947 led to more than a thousand casualties. This snapshot captures the scene in the city's police headquarters where the 2nd Battalion's headquarters, with a flying column to assist the police, were stationed.

Above: Gone are the solar topis and shorts as the 2nd Battalion parade in India, late in 1947. The regiment earned its motto, 'Hindoostan', through almost continuous service in India from 1804. That association, which has never ended, changed forever in October 1947, when the 2nd Battalion left its camp in Bangalore, to embark at Bombay for Southampton and home.

Right: Among the papers of Sergeant F.S. Taylor of the 2nd Battalion is this snap of two Tigers, probably in Bangalore, on the eve of their departure for home, in August or September 1947. The broad grins evident here may be from nerves, as few soldiers would make light of a Mk II Sten gun.

3

NORTH AMERICA

The Royal Leicestershire Regiment's long association with the Americas began in 1757, when the 17th Foot was despatched to Halifax, Nova Scotia. The regiment was to remain in North America for ten years, fighting first the French and Spanish and then a fierce combination of native tribes led by their chief, Pontiac.

This first period of American service brought three well-earned battle honours – for the capture of Louisburg, Martinique and Havannah. It also forged a link between the regiment and James Wolfe, who died at Quebec at the head of a battalion of grenadiers, including those of the 17th Regiment. Certainly the Tigers felt the loss, adding a black line of mourning to the lace facings of their uniform, and having their band play 'Wolfe's Dirge' as their officers' call and before the National Anthem at church parades.

The 17th Regiment returned to North America in 1776. At first, fortune smiled on the British, the regiment assisting in the brilliant capture of New York and, at Princeton, driving off at bayonet-point a brigade of Washington's finest troops, which had threatened to encircle them. The following year, the rebel capital, Philadelphia, was taken and their army twice defeated. In 1779, however, the 17th Regiment formed part of the garrison of Stony Point, when it was seized by the rebels.

A misguided attempt was then made to carry the war into the southern states of America. There, despite a series of notable (yet costly) victories, Cornwallis's army was forced to surrender at Yorktown, when the arrival of a powerful French fleet temporarily wrested command of the sea from the British. The 17th Foot once again marched into captivity – though a detachment remained in camp at Kingsbridge, New York, until peace was agreed in 1783.

From 1795 until 1798 the regiment saw service in the Caribbean where an attempt was made to seize St Domingo from the French. The Tigers did not return to North America for over half a century. Then, in 1856, the 1st Battalion was posted from the Crimea to Quebec and Montreal. In 1861 the newly raised 2nd Battalion joined them, as part of the garrison of Halifax, Nova Scotia. Having sailed for home in 1865 and 1867, respectively, the Tigers did not return to North America until 1888, when the 1st Battalion was posted first to Bermuda, then to Halifax (from 1891 to 1893) and finally the West Indies, where the battalion was divided between the islands of Barbados, St Lucia and Jamaica (1893–5).

Right: The death of Wolfe at Quebec, 13 September 1759. The general fell at the head of the 'Louisburg' grenadiers, a composite battalion formed from the grenadier companies (including that of the 17th Regiment) of the brigade he had commanded at the capture of Louisburg the year before. Wolfe was clearly held in high regard and a lament in his honour was added to the regimental music.

Below: The re-enactment of the storming of Fort Moro, Cuba, at the Aldershot Tattoo in 1938. The chief Spanish settlement, Havannah, surrendered two days after the capture of the fort, in August 1762, but was returned to Spain in exchange for Florida at the peace of 1763.

Wreath laying at Stony Point in 1960. In 1955 US veterans began to commemorate the capture of the fort above the Hudson River. The regiment's wreath recalls the 19 dead, 45 wounded and 284 missing or captured of the 17th Regiment.

One of the earliest surviving records in the regiment's archives is a 1783 'state' of the 17th Regiment at Kingsbridge, New York. In 1890, the site of the camp – confirmed by finds such as buttons bearing the number '17' – was excavated by W.L. Calver of the New York Historical Society.

A general view of the site of the regiment's camp at Kingsbridge, taken in 1903. The site is apparently ideal for a military camp, being well drained and sheltered.

An officers' hut on the site of the Kingsbridge camp, excavated in 1917. A number of silver buttons were found, as well as many fragments of wine and spirit bottles!

Above: Officers of the 17th Regiment, photographed beneath the walls of either Quebec or Halifax, Nova Scotia. The uniforms and badges – a Tiger can clearly be seen above the numerals '17' on their forage caps – date this group to the regiment's period in Canada; from 1856 to 1865.

Left: A portrait of Captain H.S. Wedderburn, *c.* 1865. Wedderburn was posted to the 2nd Battalion on its formation (as an ensign) in 1858. Here he serves to illustrate the full dress of a decade later, by which time he had command of a company – perhaps in Jamaica or Canada.

'B' Company of the 1st Battalion, photographed during their period on the island of Bermuda, from 1888 to 1891. On their departure, the mayor and leading citizens recorded in an address their 'high appreciation of the exemplary conduct of the men', adding that they had 'rarely met with a regiment composed of men who have conducted themselves in such a quiet and orderly manner . . .'

Staff of the officers' mess on Bermuda, 1888. The 1st Battalion on the island numbered 18 officers and some 800 men. The officers' mess employed a liveried and uniformed staff, including local people.

A spick and span 'B' Company of the 1st Battalion, on the island of St Lucia, in 1893 or '94. Clearly the isolation of this one company as St Lucia's garrison has not had a detrimental effect upon discipline.

Although only three companies were stationed on Jamaica (from 1893 to 1895), training was not neglected. Here the signallers practise with both lamps and flags.

Relaxation on Jamaica, Easter Monday 1893. Five of this group of twelve (including a local man) have musical instruments, suggesting that the island must have been a jolly, noisy place.

In 1893 the 1st Battalion sailed from Nova Scotia to the West Indies. The headquarters and four companies were stationed on Barbados, while three companies garrisoned Jamaica and one, St Lucia. The presence of the Colours (and their large number) suggests that this photograph records the sergeants and warrant officers of the four Barbados companies – with the adjutant and (for the truly observant) a wide-eyed tiger.

Wherever the British Army went, sport inevitably followed. Undaunted by terrain or climate, the Tigers threw themselves into every conceivable leisure pursuit – both native (such as the gymkhana and big game hunting in India) and imported. Cricket may have travelled the globe with Tommy Atkins but tennis, snooker and a variety of card games, played in 'drives', flourished among their families and followers. Here, on Barbados in 1895, is the corporals' football team. They are identified as (back row) corporals W. Freeman, M. Head, W.A. Wood, W. Mordick and Lance Corporal Crowther. (Middle row) Lance Corporal Barber, Corporal Berridge (the captain) and Lance Corporal Ellis. (Front row) corporals A. Hossey, Arkinstall, T. Barnett, Lance Corporal J. Thompson and Corporal J. Newton.

4

SEVASTOPOL: SERVICE ON THE BLACK SEA

The war with Russia in 1854 proved to be a severe strain upon Britain's small, professional army. Only a few months after the invasion of the Crimea, in what had been envisaged as a swift assault on the Tsar's main naval base at Sevastopol, the British (with their French and Turkish allies) were engaged in a protracted siege. Reinforcements were sent from Gibraltar and the 17th Regiment despatched by steamship from Cork to the Rock to replace them. After barely four months in Gibraltar, the regiment itself received orders to join the army before Sevastopol.

The 17th Regiment arrived on 17 December 1854 and by Christmas Day had taken its place in the trenches. The Tigers were forced to endure the privations of the severe Crimean winter, made worse by unsuitable quarters and inadequate supplies of food and clothing. The cold, poor food and disease, with a little help from the enemy, was to kill more than a third of the army besieging Sevastopol.

On 18 June 1855 the 17th Regiment joined the assault on the Redan, a Russian strongpoint. The attack was a costly failure but earned the regiment its first Victoria Cross, awarded to Corporal Philip Smith, who repeatedly braved enemy fire to carry his wounded comrades to safety. A second attempt on the Redan was also repulsed but a simultaneous French attack on the Malakoff succeeded and the following day, 9 September 1855, the Russians abandoned Sevastopol.

A month later, the regiment once again boarded transports, for an expedition against Kinburn, a fortress guarding the Nikolaev naval base. Naval might proved enough to reduce the fortress, however, which surrendered before troops could be landed. The Tigers were employed in removing the military supplies and guns of Kinburn, and then Sevastopol, before boarding transports once more – this time for Canada.

The sixteen-month campaign had cost the 17th Regiment 32 officers and 416 men dead or invalided home.

Officers of the 17th Regiment in the Crimea, 1855, gathered around their white-bearded Brigadier McPherson. The variety and informality of dress shows how the need for warmth and paucity of supplies had triumphed over regulations.

Captain John L. Croker with his servant, photographed in the early spring of 1855. Croker was killed in the failed assault on the Redan on 18 June 1855, as Corporal John Dexter recalled: 'my Captain, poor fellow, who was killed by my side, said, "men lie down it is impossible to advance," we lay down and our Captain told us to keep on our bellies . . . a round of grape came and struck us, and killed my Captain and 5 of the other 6 men, leaving myself and another only . . . I scarcely thought a sparrow could live . . .'

Opposite, bottom: Roger Fenton's photograph, taken in the spring of 1854, shows the white-bearded Colonel Philip McPherson – who had arrived as commanding officer of the 17th Regiment – but soon after been promoted to command the 1st Brigade of the 4th Division. With McPherson are four captains of the Leicesters: C.H.J. Heigham (the adjutant), Croker, Swire and, seated in the tent's entrance, C. McPherson, the general's son. Standing reading is the Brigade-major, Captain C.H. Earle, of the 57th Regiment.

This view of Sevastopol from the Allied lines late in 1855 shows the nature of warfare in the Crimea. Here are the trenches, which zig-zag back and forth, creeping ever closer to the Russian defences. Careful examination will reveal ghostly figures in the middle ground, barely noticed in this long exposure photograph. The city has fallen and out in 'no-man's land' a fatigue party is at work.

Visitors to the regimental museum in the 1950s examine a Russian Imperial Eagle, removed by soldiers of the 17th Foot from one of the dockyard buildings in Sevastopol. The bird still survives and can be seen in Leicester's Newarke Houses Museum.

5

NORTH AFRICA & THE MIDDLE EAST

The regiment's first posting in the Middle East was from 1841 to 1845, when a 'wing' of four companies, plus the headquarters, was stationed in Aden. This small outpost, vital for coaling and watering ships en route to India, proved unhealthy and dangerous; the 17th Regiment losing men to both Arab pirates and the merciless climate.

In 1889, the 2nd Battalion spent another year in Aden on their way home from Burma, returning for a further two years' service in Egypt in 1900. The Tigers next set foot in the Middle East in December 1915. Landing near Basra, the 2nd Battalion joined the force gathering for the relief of Kut-el-Amara, in Mesopotamia (now Iraq). Although Kut was to fall before help arrived, the Leicestershire Regiment battled on up the Tigris, driving the Turks beyond Baghdad. The campaign proved just as costly as those of the Western Front; disease and the climate proving to be far more deadly than Turkish bullets.

In January 1918, the 2nd Battalion was withdrawn, first to Egypt, and then to join Allenby's offensive in Palestine. The 2nd Leicesters, with the 7th (Meerut) Division, advanced along the Mediterranean coast, contending as much against the terrain as the enemy, and sweeping up hundreds of Turkish, German and even Austrian prisoners. From Arsuf the Tigers pushed northwards up the coast, their victorious march carrying them, in a growing dust-cloud, through Acre and Beirut and on to Homs and Tripoli.

The 1st Battalion spent three peaceful years in Egypt from 1924 until 1927. The same cannot be said of the 2nd Battalion's stay in the Sudan at the same time, which coincided with a violent outbreak among Egyptian units in the garrison at Khartoum and along the Nile.

The 2nd Leicesters were to return to Palestine in September 1938, as part of Britain's response to the Arab Revolt; deploying aircraft, radios and military intelligence against nomadic groups who replied with sniping and roadside bombs. By the time of the battalion's departure in September 1940 (to face the Italians in the Western Desert), the insurgency was over and the military effort devoted to winning over the local tribes with get-togethers, film shows and fireworks.

The war that followed was a far more serious affair. For nearly a year, save for a forlorn attempt to hold Crete against a German airborne assault, the 2nd and 2/5th Battalions remained in North Africa. Deployed in the Western Desert, then in Palestine, Syria and Tunisia, the Leicesters faced first the Italians, then the Vichy French, and finally Rommel's Afrika Korps in the trenches around Tobruk.

Just as the 2nd Battalion was fated to bid farewell to British India, the 1st Battalion was the last posted to the Sudan, taking part in the final parades in Khartoum as the country received its independence in 1955.

The best shots of the 2nd Battalion in Alexandria, 1902. Lieutenant and Quartermaster W.F. Hammond sits at the centre, flanked by Band Master Thompson (left) and Colour-Sergeant Pursey (right). Behind are sergeants Garbutt, Armston, Thornburn, Arkinstall and Freeman.

The guard room of the 2nd Battalion at Alexandria. It is interesting to note the additional ventilation (both above and below).

The camp of the 2nd Battalion beside the sea in Egypt in 1902. Life under canvas (with a sea breeze) has its appeal – especially in a hot climate. It can also often be a misery. In 1939 the 2nd Battalion enjoyed bathing trips to Jaffa and Tel Aviv but a generation later, on Cyprus, conditions were far more basic – with special soap issued for shaving in sea water!

The 'RP' brassards (if not their general demeanour) identify these men as the 2nd Battalion's Regimental Provost Sergeant and his Regimental Police. Internal discipline for the battalion was in their hands, directed by the Regimental Sergeant Major.

A battalion, like any large organisation, needs a large variety of skills to function efficiently. In addition to clerks, policemen, signallers, and the like, there are many trades required – from cobblers and tailors, to printers and (as here) carpenters or joiners. This is the 2nd Battalion's woodworkers' bench, at Alexandria in 1902. *(Courtesy of Squire de Lisle)*

More of the tradesmen required to keep a battalion smart and active. It seems wrong to divide these tradesmen but these are actually the tailors of the 2nd Battalion in Colchester in 1905.

A remarkable photograph taken from the 2nd Battalion's lines, possibly through a trench periscope, of the bombardment of the strong Turkish position at Sanniyat, on the River Tigris, late December 1917.

Turkish prisoners taken by the 2nd Battalion in Mesopotamia, 1917. Captain Donald Weir of the 2nd Battalion admired the Turks, 'the Turk . . . has really up to date behaved quite decently,' but he did not like the country, 'It is getting just devilish hot and the flies and mosquitoes really awful.'

Few soldiers (from Napoleon onwards) posted to Egypt can resist a trip to the Pyramids. These are believed to be lads of the 2nd Battalion, pausing in Egypt en route for Palestine in January 1918.

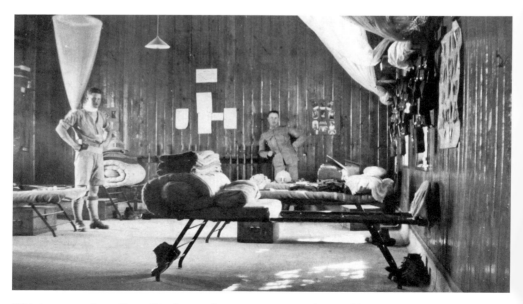

'This is a snap of our Room I took one afternoon just to see if it would come out alright [sic] not too bad is it.' A 2nd Battalion barrack room at Ismailia, Egypt, in 1924.

Guard mounting by a detachment of the 2nd Battalion on the Suez Canal near Ismailia, 1924.

If the 2nd Battalion imagined that their posting to Khartoum in 1923 would be a quiet one, they were swiftly disabused. Growing nationalism in both Egypt and the Sudan led to violent outbreaks among both Egyptian and Sudanese troops, which severely stretched the already widely spread detachments of the Tigers. On 27 November 1924 the Tigers were just in time to guard the vital Blue Nile Bridge at Khartoum.

Detachments of the 2nd Battalion were rushed to a number of vulnerable points. At the Egyptian Military Hospital, Sudanese troops murdered three doctors and a sergeant of the RAMC. Captain Tunks, leading a scratch force of bandsmen, restored order but died later from a wound in the throat. Here men of 'D' Company stand guard.

In October 1927, the 1st Battalion came second in the Command's rifle competition. Here, the crack shots of 'A' Company show off their medals (and their Lewis Gun).

Army life in peacetime was often a family affair. This is the 1st Battalion's Married Families' Swimming Sports, at Alexandria in 1927. While the wives and children splash, the battalion band plays appropriate music.

After nearly a year's service in Palestine, attempting to combat the Arab rising, the 2nd Battalion had reached a peak of efficiency, using local intelligence and radios to coordinate air support, while also waging an almost Wild West guerrilla war of sniping, road-side bombs and frantic car chases. Here platoon commanders coordinate a sweep through Arab settlements.

Service in Palestine was, for the 2nd Battalion, a mixture of modern guerrilla war and old-fashioned colonial policing. During the battalion's fifteen months in Palestine, four privates were killed in action and seven wounded. Six others were killed in motoring or shooting accidents, in most cases a result of difficult and unfamiliar terrain and duties. It was an arduous tour of duty too, with the battalion so under-strength that no section was spared; even the battalion's band and drums leaping aboard their vehicles to act as an escort to ration parties and the ever-ready flying column.

A Bren gun of the 2nd Battalion in Palestine. The battalion was not used solely against the Arab population. In October 1939, a company was deployed in the Nahariya district, where a new Jewish settlement had sprung up.

Despite newsreel film of light tanks and other vehicles tearing through the Libyan desert, the infantrymen of the 2nd and 2/5th Battalions marched through the sand – as they always had done.

Two press photographs of the 2nd Battalion in Libya, 1941. News from home has always been important to keep up morale and to bring small comforts and gifts. Having been in the front line around Tobruk since September 1941, the withdrawal of the German and Italian besiegers in the first week of December allowed the arrival not only of letters from loved ones but also welcome additions to the diet such as beer and captured Italian rations.

Water and mail were both in short supply in the Western Desert. All letters had to be diverted (after the Italian intervention in the war) around Africa, rather than through the Mediterranean and Suez Canal. In October 1940 the then Secretary of State for War, Anthony Eden, visited the 2nd Battalion near Matruh and promised an improvement. Water, however, remained a problem – as did a satisfactory means of conveying it, until the large, rigid German (or 'Jerry') cans were adopted. At Tobruk, the 2nd Battalion were reduced to nocturnal visits from water carriers and long, dry days in between in which a single water bottle had to suffice.

Two photographs recording different aspects of the 1st Battalion's service in the Sudan, during the last six months of British rule from April to October 1955. Above is an inspection in Khartoum by the Governor, Sir Knox Helm. Below we see one of many training exercises taking advantage of the boundless emptiness of the Sudan.

6

SOUTH AFRICA

Although it is the Defence of Ladysmith which has come to symbolise the Leicesters' war in South Africa, the 118-day siege was merely one incident in a series of gruelling campaigns which involved troops from both regular battalions, the volunteers and militia.

The 1st Battalion had arrived in South Africa in 1895, serving first in Cape Town and then Pietermaritzburg, the capital of Natal. There the battalion was soon augmented with a strong mounted infantry company and schooled in the new kind of warfare to be expected on the veldt.

The 1st Battalion served throughout the war, from the first shots, fired by a piquet of the Leicesters posted above the Glencoe camp in October 1899, until peace was signed in 1902. It was a long and hard war. Over 250 soldiers of the battalion remained beyond their original terms of service and the total casualties amounted to 3 officers and 122 NCOs and men.

The Tigers performed well in the early set-piece engagements (at Talana Hill, Laing's Nek and Belfast) and later played their part in the guerrilla war which followed, guarding convoys and dashing in pursuit of elusive Boer commandos. The peace found them spread out along a blockhouse line between Standerton and Blesbok Spruit.

The 1st Battalion photographed at Wynberg, shortly after their arrival in Natal early in 1896. A fascinating record of the battalion; with the pioneers, drums and band, as well as the infantry companies all clearly visible. Most unusually the troops are in shirt-sleeve order, a rare sight in Victorian photographs.

A British regiment has often been compared to a family. Sometimes this was literally true. Here Private Smith of the 1st Battalion stands beside the grave of his brother at Pietermaritzburg, Natal, *c.* 1898.

The 1st Battalion's football team in Natal, *c.* 1897. The battalion's star player, Private W. Cox, sits almost concealed by the trophy. Cox left South Africa just before the outbreak of war but returned as a reservist on 1 March 1900.

A section of the 1st Battalion's mounted infantry company, on the eve of war, 1899. Two years earlier, the battalion had taken delivery of 137 Argentine ponies to form the company. The Leicesters' first casualties of the war were from the M.I. company; a Boer shell fired from Talana Hill killing Lieutenant William Hannah and wounding Farrier Sergeant Shepherd (attached from the 18th Hussars) and Private Woods. Once besieged in Ladysmith, the company was attached to the troops guarding the cattle and draught oxen of the garrison.

Another fascinating photograph of the entire 1st Battalion at Ladysmith on the eve of war in 1899. The battalion is deployed behind Colonel G.D. Carleton, mounted on his grey, Felix. To the left are the band and drums, with the battalion's machine gun on its mule-drawn carriage. Behind is the transport and to the right, the mounted infantry company led by Captain Sherer, on their hardy, Argentine ponies.

The retreat from Dundee, after the inconclusive battle of Talana Hill. The regiment's mounted infantry, exhausted by the long march in appalling weather, have just reached the safety of Ladysmith. Corporal Lionel Dowding described the withdrawal, 'As we started to march it started to rain and continued to rain all night. The road in some parts was up to our knees in mud. Some of the transport kept getting stuck which kept halting the column and delayed us a lot. Whenever the troops had to wait a few minutes they kept dropping off to sleep.'

Although taken at The Curragh, in Ireland, this photograph records the draft from 'B' Company of the 2nd Battalion chosen in May 1899 to reinforce the 1st Battalion in South Africa. The draft has already been issued with their sun helmets and khaki drill uniforms.

Forced to abandon their camp and withdraw into Ladysmith, the 1st Battalion lost all but what they could carry – leaving behind stores, equipment, and even their drums (one of which can now be seen in the regimental museum). The officers found themselves without even plates and cutlery with which to eat. Here, Lieutenant-Colonel G.D. Carleton and Major E.R. Scott (talking to his servant) make do with deck chairs and a shelter made from corrugated iron.

Entrusted with holding Cove Redoubt and Gordon Post on the northern perimeter of the Ladysmith defences, the 1st Battalion hastily constructed stone 'sangars' and dug trenches in the rocky soil. Here is the battalion headquarters, built from the red sandstone of the area. The Boers did not prosecute a vigorous siege – relying more on starvation to bring surrender. With a wry nod towards the enemy's well-known religious fervour, Private T. Horne noted of their artillery bombardment: 'Although they have a good many guns mounted, and have fired hundreds of tons of shells into our camp [they] have done little damage. I think they must point the guns towards the town and fire, and trust to God to guide them.'

The armoured train at Ladysmith, 1899. For the first few weeks of the siege, Ladysmith's commander, Sir George White, maintained the fiction that his was a field force rather than a beleaguered garrison. One company of the 1st Battalion played its part by manning an armoured train, kept with steam up at the station, ready to sally out at a moment's notice to strike at the encircling Boers.

'D' Section Reserves for South Africa. The declaration of war in South Africa and early military setbacks led to the mobilisation of reservists. These old soldiers, called back to the Colours to teach the Boers a lesson, are to join the 1st Battalion – already besieged in Ladysmith.

The early setbacks in South Africa led to the mobilisation of the empire against the two Boer republics. Reservists were swiftly despatched and a Volunteer Service Company was formed from the unmarried men of the 1st (Volunteer) Battalion, under Captain William Augustus Harrison (seen here seated – to the right).

By the end of November 1901, the 1st Battalion was strung-out, as the garrison of a line of blockhouses, between Standerton and Ermelo in the Transvaal. Life in the blockhouses was clearly generally dull. 'You are quite right', Private Alfred Burrows wrote home on 7 January 1902, 'the troops in the blockhouses are having a dreary time of it, day after day, week after week, & month after month they look upon the world, represented to <u>them</u> by the four walls of the blockhouse & a bare ridge in front.'

A garrison of the Leicesters beside their blockhouse at Standerton, 1901. 'The blockhouse (or "fort")', recalled Private Burrows, 'is a structure of galvanised iron in the form of a letter O, with two layers of iron filled with small stones as a protection against bullets, a few loopholes, & a rocky floor upon which to sleep. Outside it is surrounded by a network of barbed wire, which by the way, is the most fiendish article of commerce ever invented & which causes more bad language than any other thing.'

Two photographs of men of the 1st Battalion in South Africa, which illustrate the changes wrought by the war. Left is Private Simpson, photographed in Treadway's studio in Ladysmith on the eve of the war. Below is Corporal Smith. Unfortunately, we cannot positively identify either man. The medal rolls show four private Simpsons and though there is only one S. Smith, he is recorded as a private rather than a corporal. Simpson is in the red tunic and blue trousers of the peacetime soldier. Corporal Smith's is the durable khaki serge (rather than khaki drill which proved unsatisfactory) and slouch or Terai hat which was another response to harsh wartime conditions.

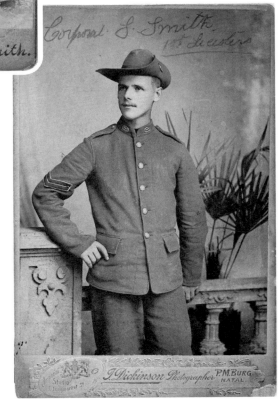

Two views of the return of the Volunteer Service Company from South Africa to the Glen Parva depot on 22 May 1901. Captain Harrison leads his men, his head bowed in conversation with an officer from the depot. In fact, the day proved to be less than perfect. Having travelled up from Southampton, the volunteers missed their connection at St Pancras and had to catch a later train which did not stop at South Wigston. A special then carried them back from Leicester for a low-key march to the depot; prompting one old volunteer to observe, 'it looks as though we were glad to get rid of them, and very sorry to see them back again.'

The unveiling of the South African War Memorial in Town Hall Square, Leicester, on 14 July 1909. Field Marshal Lord Grenfell is about to remove the Union flags, revealing J.C. McClure's sculptures of 'War' and 'Grief' on either side of 'Peace'. The memorial might have been very different indeed, as the War Memorial Committee had originally engaged Alfred Gilbert who began work on a 'colossal' figure of Victory. After nearly five years of delay and prevarication, the committee's representative, J.A. Corah, visited Gilbert's Bruges studio and reported that there was little hope of ever seeing a finished sculpture. The committee swiftly raised yet more funding and commissioned McClure, who proved reliable if less adventurous than Gilbert. A party from the 1st Battalion travelled up from Kent, attending the unveiling and lodging their old Colours in St Martin's Church on the same day.

The Defence of Ladysmith remains a source of legitimate pride for the Tigers. An annual ball was held on the anniversary of the relief (28 February) each year and the surviving defenders would often gather to discuss the campaign. On 28 February 1914, those veterans of the siege still serving with the 1st Battalion were photographed together at Fermoy.

7

THE WESTERN FRONT: FRANCE & FLANDERS

Despite years of service throughout the empire, there is no doubt that the Leicestershire Regiment saw its bloodiest fighting on the arc of battlefields which runs through Flanders into France. With the exception of the 2nd Battalion's service in the Middle East, it was here that all the regular, territorial and service battalions fought during the First World War.

Between 1914 and 1918 no fewer than fourteen Tigers battalions fought on the Western Front, with a further seven specially raised at home to train troops – or provide garrisons to release fitter men – for active service. It was an experience that was to shape the twentieth century and which still influences our views of war and military service.

A generation later it was on the Western Front that the 2/5th was to fight in 1940 and across which the new 1st (ex 8th) Battalion was to advance from Normandy into Holland in 1944 and 1945.

As an appendix, it is appropriate to add Norway to this theatre of war. In 1940 the territorials of the 1/5th Battalion joined the doomed attempt to forestall a Nazi conquest of Norway. Blunders and missed opportunities could not be offset by the courage and fighting spirit of the Allied forces in Norway and many Tigers were killed, captured, or forced to seek refuge in neutral Sweden.

The 1st Battalion's machine gunners in action on the River Aisne in mid-September 1914. Trench warfare was still a matter for the future but this team have taken cover behind a hedge amid the tall grass of late summer.

Left: The 1st Battalion's transport somewhere in France, September 1914. Success in the first month of the war came as much from boots as bullets, as the Allied and German armies sought to out-manoeuvre one another. One advantage of marching with the transport was that rifles could be stowed on the wagons.

Below: The beginnings of trench warfare. Men of Lieutenant A. Weyman's No. 5 Platoon, 1st Leicester's 'B' Company, have scraped cover from themselves, somewhere near Vailly-sur-Aisne, in mid-September 1914.

Above: Another view of 'B' company's scraped entrenchment at Vailly-sur-Aisne, in September 1914. This old soldier may have crawled in for a smoke but his SMLE rifle remains close at hand and though its butt may be muddy, the breech and barrel will be 'clean, bright and slightly oiled'.

Right: Captain John C. Baines, adjutant of the 2/4th Battalion, obligingly shows us the dress and equipment of an officer of 1914 or 1915. Baines was a committed territorial, receiving his captaincy in 1909 – a year after the formation of the Territorial Force.

Above: The headgear of these men, a
mixture of 'caps-comforter' trench
caps and field service caps, show
the adaptations of trench warfare.
A scribbled note on the back of this
photograph identifies these men
as machine gunners of the 1st
Battalion's 'B' Company at Rue de Bois
in 1915.

Left: Another scene on the Rue
de Bois, 1915. While his sergeant
prepares breakfast, a private of the 1st
Battalion indulges in a little sniping.
Only just visible to the left is Sergeant
Cunningham, who (a note tells us)
was shortly afterwards killed by
shrapnel.

Men of one of the service battalions rest, while their officers confer, August 1915. Lieutenant C.A.B. Elliott of the 8th Battalion noted in his dairy for 5 August, 'Marched on to Eecke . . . and bivouacked in field of farm. Farm very dirty and owner who talked Flemish very fast inclined to be inhospitable. We could hear the guns quite clearly in the evening.'

The rigours of active service have always led to a more flexible attitude to dress regulations. A glance at the officers of the 17th Regiment in the Crimea shows a fine array of beards and rabbit-skin 'bunny' jackets rather than red coats. Here, sixty years later, men of an unidentified battalion await their move up to the front line. Most wear the comfortable and practical (but decidedly unmilitary) 'Cap, winter, Service Dress' which was swiftly christened the 'Gor Blimey' by its grateful wearers.

Men of the 4th Battalion covering their newly issued steel helmets with sacking, some time in 1916.

Company Sergeant Major Edward Perkins of the 7th Battalion, who died on 18 July 1916, from wounds received at Bazentin-le-Petit. The capture of Bazentin-le-Petit Wood by the service battalions of the regiment on 14 July 1916 was undoubtedly one of the finest achievements of the Somme campaign. Just before dawn the four battalions of the 110th Brigade stormed the German lines, seizing Bazentin Wood save for a few pockets of resistance. German machine guns and a bombardment from their artillery cost the attackers dear, however. The 7th Battalion's War Diary records, 'Our total casualties were 18 officers & 535 men killed & wounded . . . Next morning about 100 men answered the Roll.'

A fascinating record of the 6th Battalion at rest on the Somme in 1916. These are the men who took Bazentin Wood in the daring pre-dawn attack on 14 July. Here they enjoy a well-earned rest, with piled SMLE rifles. Note too the stencilled tiger on their helmet covers.

Men of the 11th battalion, the 'Midland Pioneers', pausing for tea and a smoke near Zillebeke, during the Third Battle of Ypres, 2 August 1917.

Two views taken by Tigers of their living conditions in 1916. Left is 'Lulu Lane' and below, 'a trench in the salient' near Ypres. Lulu Lane is a deeply dug trench, supported with revetments and sandbags. The lower view is of a trench around Ypres, where the high water table prevented deep digging and led to a reliance on sandbag ramparts for protection. Rain or shellfire, neither of which was in short supply, could ruin days of work in a single night. As Dick Read, of the 8th Battalion, recalled, 'Every now and then, huge slices of the trench sides slipped down to the bottom, loosened by the alternate frosts, rains and thaws . . . the thaw had flooded the trench floor, and in places the duckboard sump covers had floated off. Where earth from the sides had fallen, we unsuspecting unfortunates blundered in up to the waist.'

Bazentin Wood, photographed on 2 September 1917. More blasted heath than French 'bois', the photographer's visit was already something of a pilgrimage, recording the scene of the Service Battalions' triumph on 14 July 1916.

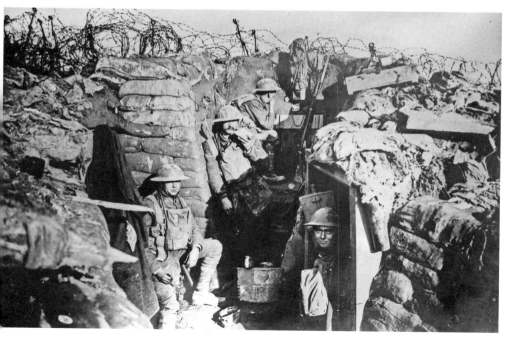

A typical scene of the First World War? Givenchy, in January 1918. The mud, the trench, barbed wire, and cheerful 'Tommies' at rest and on guard.

Lieutenant-Colonel G. German DSO with officers of the 2/5th Battalion enjoying a lull in the fighting for Passchendaele, 1 October 1917. Identified with German (clean-shaven in the foreground) are 2nd lieutenants Dakin, Scales and Green and Captain Gough.

The 1st Battalion on the Hindenburg Line, 20 November 1917. The War Diary records, 'the attack was very successful. The tanks breached very strong belts of wire with ease and the following infantry had no difficulties in passing through gaps made. The enemy appeared to be taken completely by surprise.'

Right: Territorials of the 1/4th or 2/4th Battalion repairing a trench around Ypres in 1917. The reverse 'A' frames which are clearly seen here were designed to preserve a dry floor for the trench, leaving a channel for water below. Without constant repair, any enemy shellfire, heavy rain or even frost would bring down the un-revetted sides of this trench.

Below: Another world war but the same battalion. Here is an anti-aircraft gun of the 396 Light Anti-Aircraft Battery, Royal Artillery, near the Maas River, Holland, in February 1945. The old 4th Battalion was to remain an outpost of the Tigers among the Royal Artillery.

8

GERMANY

T he Armistice in 1918 and collapse of the Third Reich in 1945 were both followed by occupations by foreign forces. In 1918, the 1st Battalion of the Leicesters made its dramatic 'March to the Rhine', covering 220 miles in 24 days, to join the Army of Occupation. In 1945, the same battalion advanced from Holland to Iserlohn in Westphalia, then Paderborn and Lingen, where the pacification of Germany and establishment of law and order became the priorities.

The Leicesters also served with both post-war armies of occupation and (after the beginning of the Cold War) defence of West Germany. To prove history's penchant for repetition, the regiment therefore joined the British Army on the Rhine in both its incarnations: the 2nd Battalion at Königstein from 1927 to 1929, and the 1st Battalion of the (since 1946) *Royal* Leicestershire Regiment once more at Iserlohn. Both postings proved to be happy ones, the troops enjoying well-equipped barracks and good relations with the local population.

2nd Lieutenant Drummond leads the advance party out of Givenchy barracks in Königstein for the last time in 1929. The scene is also being captured by Lieutenant Bolland, who stands with his camera to the right.

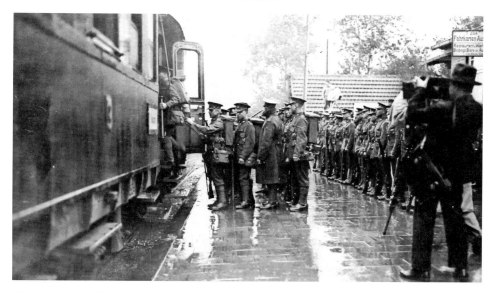

The main body of the 2nd Battalion leaving Königstein, 1929. The Tigers were the first British unit to leave the Rhine Army for home. The troops were soaked by torrential rain within minutes of leaving their barracks.

This posed farewell scene, as the loading party of the 2nd Battalion completes its work with the assistance of their German railway staff, suggests that relations were not strained in 1929. Here a Tigers corporal shakes hands with the station master.

The 2nd Battalion, freed from the Rhine Army at Oostende, en route for Dover. Colonel Creagh, commanding the battalion, observed to a local reporter, 'Germany is fine but we are all glad to be back again.'

In November 1952 the 1st Battalion returned to Germany, this time as part of number 5 Brigade of the 2nd Infantry division of the British Army of the Rhine. To the veterans of Korea, the transfer to a comfortable barracks in a peaceful, modern countryside was a welcome change. Germany also brought a concentration on training, drill and manoeuvres – as the Support Company here demonstrates.

The 1st Battalion's headquarters at Mons Barracks, Iserlohn. Built just before the war to accommodate a German anti-aircraft unit, the facilities at Iserlohn were superior, almost luxurious even, to British standards let alone what had been experienced in the Far East – in Hong Kong and Korea. The barracks were comfortable and equipped with kitchens boasting every conceivable type of culinary aid. The sports facilities were also superb, with a vast gymnasium and parade square. There was no excuse for any lack of fitness or failure on the assault course – as seen below.

Iserlohn also offered excellent facilities for the battalion's motor transport, reinforcing the role of vehicles in the type of warfare practised in Germany. The mortar team above has deployed beside its transport.

There was a new standard of smartness expected in the British Army on the Rhine, which may have come as a shock to those fresh from Korea. The tour of duty at Iserlohn gave several opportunities for the Battalion to show its skills too. On 2 June 1953 the battalion paraded in honour of the Coronation of Queen Elizabeth II (as in the lower snapshot). The lowest shot is of the Battalion led by Lieutenant-Colonel Hutchins and Major Romilly. In July 1954, the battalion also paraded to receive new Colours, from the Colonel of the Regiment, Lieutenant-General Sir Colin Callender.

9

ITALY & GREECE

As we have already seen, in May 1941 the Leicesters' 2nd Battalion was switched (at the height of its victorious campaign in North Africa) to bolster the defences of Crete. The German assault on Crete came principally from the air and should have been repulsed. The first day of the invasion did cost the Germans dear, the Leicesters playing their part by holding their position around Heraklion. Large numbers of German paratroops were killed as they landed and seven troop carrying aircraft brought down. However, blunders elsewhere gave the invaders the airfield they needed to land reinforcements (at Maleme) and by the end of May, the island had been evacuated and the Tigers returned to Egypt.

The collapse of Mussolini's Italy in September 1943 had led to the invasion of Italy. Hopes that the 2/5th Battalion's arrival on the Salerno beachhead would be a triumphal march northwards were dashed, however, when, almost from the start, fierce German resistance was encountered. Until December 1944 the 2/5th Battalion, as part of the 46th Division, fought its way northwards through Italy, battering its way through a succession of superbly positioned German defence lines in some of the hardest fighting of the war.

In December the battalion was flown to Greece, where the withdrawal of the Germans had left a power vacuum. Attempts to limit Communist influence led to bloodshed between former allies, with the Leicesters too often under fire on the streets around Athens and then Piraeus.

Such thankless police work was to characterise much of the 1st Battalion's tour of duty on Cyprus from October 1955 until May 1958. The otherwise idyllic posting was marred by the activities of EOKA, the Cypriots fighting for union with Greece. The counter-terrorism campaign involved the Tigers in patrols, raids, curfews, and the variety of security measures which was to become all-too familiar in the late twentieth century. Seventeen Tigers died while Britain and the UN wrangled over the future of the island with Greece and Turkey.

A snapshot taken from the Leicesters' lines, near Heraklion, Crete. A Luftwaffe plane falls from the sky in flames, while parachutists attract heavy fire from below.

More German parachutists descend near Heraklion, 20 May 1941. Paradoxically, while their heavy losses convinced Hitler to abandon airborne landings, the Allies were persuaded of their value.

Once again, the immediacy of the scene justifies poorer photography as men of the 2/5th Battalion race past a knocked-out German tank in their advance through Italy, c. 1944.

The River Volturno was crossed by the 2/5th Battalion on the night of 12/13 October 1943. The Leicesters waded through chest-deep water under German machine gun fire to secure the farther bank. Here are the following carriers while vital supplies were ferried across by the Royal Engineers.

The arrival of men of the
1st Battalion in Famagusta,
Cyprus, October 1955.
After the sweltering heat of
the Sudan, the posting to a
Mediterranean island might
have seemed a tonic but for
the growing local demand for
British withdrawal and union
with Greece.

Major P.G. Bligh's jeep, on escort duty, leads a convoy away from the central police station, Famagusta.

While on Cyprus the 1st Battalion received another visit from the Regiment's Colonel, Sir Colin Callender KBE, CB, MC. The general here addresses Sergeant Kelly of 'B' Company, while Captain Creagh and 2nd Lieutenant A.J. Bettles look on.

10

THE FAR EAST: MALAYA, HONG KONG, KOREA, BRUNEI & BORNEO (& AUSTRALIA)

U nconventionally, we shall begin this account of the 17th Regiment's service in the Far East with their sojourn in Australia from 1831 to 1836. Travelling out in small detachments as guards aboard convict ships bound for New South Wales and Van Diemen's Land, the regiment spent five years spread over a number of stations, the troops acting as policemen and guards for remote settlements.

The Tigers did not return to the Pacific and South China Sea for another century. In 1941 the 1st Battalion was moved from India to bolster the defences of the Malayan Peninsula and Singapore. The collapse of Britain's far eastern empire is well known – but the courage of the Leicesters, both in action alongside remnants of the 2nd East Surrey Regiment as 'The British Battalion' and throughout their long captivity as prisoners of the Japanese, cannot be too often repeated.

In May 1949 the 1st Battalion (which was in fact nearly half made up from National Servicemen) arrived aboard the *Empire Haladale* for service in Hong Kong. After nearly a year and a half on the Chinese border, the battalion was then transferred for active service in Korea as part of the United Nations force. The campaign proved a hard fought one, costing the Tigers 55 dead, 167 wounded and at least 26 taken prisoner; the tenacity of the enemy making a cruel combination with the harsh winter and difficult terrain of Korea.

The Leicesters returned to Hong Kong in 1963, once again offering support for 'internal security' and border defence. In June 1963, however, the Tigers were switched to East Malaysia where a post-imperial conflict with Indonesian insurgents was fought out through jungle, mountains and swamps.

As the 'Confrontation' came to an end in 1964, so too did the Royal Leicestershire Regiment; the 1st Battalion returning to the United Kingdom to swap their Tiger badge for that of 4th (Leicestershire) Battalion the Royal Anglian Regiment on 1 September.

Above: Bound for the east! Men of the 1st Battalion march through South Wigston on the first leg of their journey to Hong Kong in 1949.

Left: The 1st Battalion here crowds the railway platform at South Wigston, awaiting their train for Southampton and Hong Kong, 1949.

A patrol of the 1st Battalion in Korea (above). The 1st Battalion arrived in Korea, at the port of Pusan, on 13 October 1951. The under strength battalion, with nearly half its men National Servicemen, joined the Commonwealth Division south of the Imjin River. Conditions were harsh – both weather and terrain. The enemy also proved dogged and determined. Support at home resulted in a fundraising concert at the Palace Theatre on 30 March 1952 (right). The ever smiling Brigadier H.S. Pinder, then Colonel of the Regiment (into which he had been commissioned in 1908), clearly enjoyed the occasion, despite the stony face of Jack Warner – though perhaps it was Frankie Howerd, just visible behind, who was the source of the amusement.

The arrival of the 1st Battalion in Borneo. Left, men of the Headquarters Company disembark from their airliner at Labuan Island in September 1963. Below, stores arrive by a more traditional means of transport. Having arrived from Hong Kong by air, the various companies were deployed by twin-engine plane, boat and helicopter – a far cry from the days of transports and bullock carts.

From 5 to 15 December 1963 the battalion
took part in Operation Inglenook, one of the
last active service operations of the regiment.
Planned to intercept a major incursion
from Indonesia, the operation succeeded
only in deterring the raid and capturing
a considerable quantity of weaponry and
other supplies. Lieutenant-Colonel P.C.B.
Badger's comments in his war diary sum up
the situation: 'this operation cannot be said
to have been a howling success; but neither
was it a complete failure. The enemy did not
achieve his probable aim . . . and his main
party was dispersed, harried and departed . . .
leaving a quantity of ammunition, equipment
and documents.' Right, a Tiger models the
shoulder flash of an Indonesian invader,
while trophies, including mortar bombs and
grenades, are displayed below.

Above: Once again, the terrain in Brunei and British North Borneo proved a major challenge, the 1st Battalion relying upon boats and helicopters for swift movement, supply and intelligence. Despite the fact that one major ambush had been triggered prematurely by the unexpected arrival of a support helicopter, Lieutenant-Colonel Badger was quick to report, 'there can never be too many or ever enough helicopters.' Borneo was certainly the shape of things to come.

Left: 2nd Lieutenant M.J. Peele, whose Military Cross, for a series of actions from 23 to 26 January 1964, was the last gallantry medal awarded to a soldier of the Royal Leicestershire Regiment.

11

COME ON THE TIGERS!

This then is the family album of the Royal Leicestershire Regiment. Sadly, like all family albums it has gaps and images which do not adequately tell our story. The Tigers have suffered severe losses as far as their records are concerned. On 17 March 1840 the right wing and headquarters of the 17th Regiment embarked on the transport *Hannah* for conveyance from Karachi (or Kurrachee as they knew it) to Mumbai (Bombay). At nine that night the *Hannah* ran aground on a sandbank and though all lives were saved, as the *Bombay Gazette* reported the catastrophe, 'the clothing of the 17th Regiment is all lost, and the arms and accoutrements either lost or ruined. Treasure and mess plate have shared the same fate . . .' No mention is made of the regiment's records but they too had gone in a swirl of muddy water.

In the debacle of Malaya in 1941, the 1st Battalion's records were once again lost. Even the Colours, the most precious objects of any battalion, were abandoned; left for safe-keeping, with some Mess Silver, in a Penang Bank. Though the King's Colour was later recovered, it is not surprising that the gallantly-fought campaign of Jitra, Kampar and the withdrawal towards Singapore – followed as it was by three bitter years of captivity and shameful inhumanity on the part of their captors – have not left a rich archival record.

This story has been illustrated from the photographic collections of the regiment and of the Record Office for Leicestershire, Leicester & Rutland. There are many gaps, which must be filled (and perhaps will be with your help!).

The collection is rich enough, however, to convey the story of the Tigers, from the earliest days in India to the rifle range at Glen Parva – from the days of powdered wigs and ramrods to Universal Carriers and webbing gaiters. This collection shows, if it shows anything, that a regiment is a family – with a family likeness, with traditions and customs, and with a story to be told.

The rallying cry of Colonel Philip Bent VC, as he led the 9th Battalion into the attack on Polygon Wood in January 1917, will serve as well as any, 'Come on, The Tigers!'

Two sets of gates, both of which represent the regiment. Above is the main gate into the depot at Glen Parva on the eve of its closure forever. For how many recruits was this the first glimpse of army life? Below is the gate into the War Memorial on Leicester's Victoria Park. The photograph was taken on 21 June 1975, when a memorial overthrow, commemorating 'the service and sacrifice' of all Tigers, whether of the 17th Foot or Royal Leicestershire Regiment, was unveiled.

To many, it is the Colours which embody
the spirit of the regiment. In the past,
they were carried on the battlefield –
passed from hand to hand as ensigns and
then colour-sergeants fell – serving as a
rallying point and marking the centre of
the battalion. The Colours embody much
of the regiment's history too, bearing
the battle honours and badge, as well as
showing (on the Regimental Colour) the
colour once worn on cuffs and uniform
'facings' to identify the 17th Foot from
its neighbours in the line. Above are the
Colours of the 2nd Battalion at Alexandria
in 1926. Right is Lieutenant M.W.
McD. Cairns, with the newly presented
Regimental Colour of the 1st Battalion, in
May 1953.

Above the overthrow is the badge of the regiment, a green tiger, with its motto 'Hindoostan'. Both originate in India, where the 17th Foot served for many years. Why the tiger has green stripes and why his tail is sometimes up and sometimes down (besides the obvious need to leave space for the motto) remains a tantalising mystery despite many plausible explanations.

To the public, it is often the band which represents the regiment. No parade is complete without military music – even the fifes and drums alone, without brass and woodwind, convey the martial spirit. In the seventeenth century Leicester's trained band made special payments for their drummer and his finery, and recruiting parties ever since have known the magical draw of military marches and laced uniforms for small boys of all ages. The depot band (below – playing at a depot 'at home') was always available for local civic functions and throughout the 1930s played Sunday afternoon concerts at Leicester's De Montfort Hall gardens. Sadly, the occasion above, at which a combined Fusilier and Tigers band was fielded, is unidentified.

Of course, a regiment is also its men – whether they are long-service regulars, territorials or militia, wartime conscripts or National Servicemen. All are members of the regimental 'family', an affinity which continues even after discharge or demobilisation and which draws many to join other old comrades at reunions or in the Royal Tigers Association. A generation separates the men in these photographs but their spirit is the same. Right are veterans of the First World War, sporting medal ribbons and wound stripes. Below are two lads of the 2nd Battalion in India at the end of the Second World War. They are all survivors – which is perhaps why they are also all smiling.

Two uneasy heroes. With Private Buckingham is Lance Corporal Thomas Newcombe, who received the Distinguished Conduct Medal and Russian Cross of St George (4th Class) for his attempt to save a wounded officer in May 1915. Brought back from France to aid recruitment, both Buckingham and Newcombe (seen below with another recipient of a gallantry medal, Lance Corporal Robinson) toured Leicestershire's towns and villages. At Hinckley, seen here, in February 1916, they were feted by the Volunteer Training Corps, a band, and crowds of hosiery workers. Unhappy in the limelight and making speeches written by others, Buckingham returned to the front. He was killed on the Somme in September 1916, serving with the 1st Battalion.

The Reception of Leicestershire Heroes at Hinckley, Saturday, Feb. 19th, 1916.
3 Pte. Buckingham, V.C. (front), Lce Cpl. Newcombe (right) and Lce-Cpl Robinson (le

'WOLFE'S DIRGE'

At the conclusion of Church Parade, the band or drums of the Royal Leicestershire Regiment would play 'Wolfe's Dirge', a dim recollection of those 'Louisburg Grenadiers' of the 17th Foot who stood beside James Wolfe at Quebec in 1759. It is fitting then, that our conclusion has the same name.

We have seen the Tigers as a family with a pedigree stretching back directly to a regiment raised to serve James II in 1688. The regiment has seen battalions raised and amalgamated, reduced to cadre-strength and disembodied as wars ended or ideas of warfare evolved. Different branches of the tree have intertwined, as the militia and volunteers have marched into the family home at Glen Parva and as battalions received new roles and designations – as 'Young Soldiers', and Royal Engineers or Royal Artillery anti-aircraft gunners and searchlight men.

The story of the Tigers has been (and still is being) well told by the regiment's many historians. The regiment's archives and museum may be visited at the Record Office for Leicestershire, Leicester & Rutland in Wigston Magna and Newarke Houses Museum in Leicester respectively. All the photographs here are accessible through the record office – which, like the museum, remains eager to hear from anyone who can add to its collections of documents or photographs.

Also available from The History Press

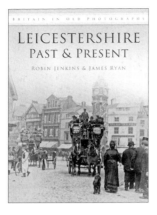

Leicestershire Past & Present

9780752465159

From the multicultural bustle of Leicester to the smaller market towns of Market Harborough and Lutterworth and even smaller picturesque villages, Leicestershire is a unique and varied county with a rich cultural heritage. *Leicestershire Past & Present* contrasts a selection of 300 old and new photographs, juxtaposed to demonstrate the changes that have occurred in the scene over the intervening years.

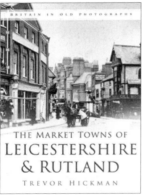

The Market Towns of Leicestershire & Rutland

9780750941372

Drawing on Trevor Hickman's unsurpassed collection of prints, engravings and photographs, this book captures bygone days in nine Leicestershire market towns. Explore towns including Market Harborough, Melton Mowbray and Leicester with the county's foremost local historian.

Leicestershire Food and Drink

9780752448633

This exploration of the county's fare sets food and drink against the character of Leicestershire to discover how history, landscape and culture have shaped the county's diet. It explains how world-renowned delicacies such as the Melton Mowbray pork pie, and both Stilton and Red Leicester cheese have made their name. With local recipes and mouth-watering photographs of the final product, this book will inspire chefs far and wide. Whether a resident of Leicestershire or merely a fan of its food and drink, this book is a must-have for all those who appreciate the fine traditions of the county's cuisine.

Visit our website and discover thousands of other History Press books.
www.thehistorypress.co.uk